# LET'S CO-OPERAT
## BY MILDRED MASHEDER

## Table of Contents

## ILLUSTRATIONS BY PETRA HUGHES

© Mildred Masheder

First published by the Peace Pledge Union in 1986

This edition published in 1997 by Green Print, an imprint of
Merlin Press Limited, 2 Rendlesham Mews
Rendlesham, Nr Woodbridge
Suffolk  IP12 2SZ

# Introduction

This booklet is addressed mainly to parents and teachers who deal with children in nursery and primary schools or playgroups. Things are seen, with great sympathy and insight, from the age range of about 3–11, and many co-operative activities are suggested.

Though Mildred Masheder writes in a language which is easy to understand, she herself is a scholar of child development and has abundant experience to draw from. The most important thing that we can take from her is that it is neither desirable nor necessary to pressurise children, whether they be our own progeny or our pupils. Have we the confidence to realise that, starting from play, they will learn to read and write – she mentions the Letter Box game – as well as discover how to co-operate with each other and gradually to extend their caring attitudes, as they grow older, to the wider community?

Upon such a basis of belonging to a group, their play will turn to artistic forms of expressing, in dance, painting, drama (including puppetry, which is mentioned) and crafts. This will not only give them pleasure but provide motives for studying the normal subjects of the primary school curriculum.

It seems to me that this booklet is disarmingly simple because it is authoritative. We can trust the author and so we can trust the children.

Anthony Weaver.
Joint co-ordinator
Peace Education Project.

## A Confession. Parents and Teachers Please Read this Before Anything Else.

On reading this book I realise how much it sounds as if this is a counsel of perfection and can be very discouraging for those of us like myself who never managed to achieve this wonderful parenting and teaching! All I can say is that I really loved my daughters and my pupils and I tried to do the best for them and fortunately children of all ages are forgiving of our constant mistakes and failures, especially when they understand the many pressures that beset us daily. Parents and teachers have the most challenging job in the world and most of us have had little preparation for it in terms of personal relationships. Let us be reassured that it is never too late and whether we feel depressed and downhearted because we feel we have failed, or whether we have never given much thought to these approaches, we can give them a try, realising that however many mistakes we make in the process, goodwill does promote good will and that we all stand to gain through these little ripples of co-operation and more peaceful conflict-solving. The progress may be slow and often would seem to be at a standstill, but if we keep on trying something good will come out of it in the long run.

My thanks to the Polytechnic of North London for giving me an Honorary Research Fellowship which helped me to carry out this project.

# LET'S CO-OPERATE

Why not co-operate? There are so many advantages: feelings of goodwill towards other people instead of being left out and isolated; no anxiety about having to win or otherwise feel a failure; getting affirmation and encouragement from others as rivalry diminishes.

This book is aimed at teachers, parents and everyone concerned with children between the ages of 3 and 11, with the purpose of building up an atmosphere in the home and the school which promotes good relationships between all concerned. This is a life-long process and the earlier we start the better: the little ripples of peace-making and co-operation can gradually be turned into great waves of confidence, trust and caring.

This is a practical book with many ideas and activities to help educators to create a climate of positive goodwill amongst the children in their care.

The most important need is to set a good example; how often do we expect young people to have standards that we ourselves do not reach! The aims and ideals hoped for in this book are equally applicable to adults as to children. The hidden messages about what is permissable behaviour for us are immediately picked up by the children and they feel that this is also right for them; whereas whatever we preach and moralise about goes unheard and unheeded. We all know this in our heart of hearts, but the old edict, 'Don't do as I do, do as I tell you', dies hard!

The best example we can give is of secure confidence, so in this case we adults should try to set the scene by nurturing our own self-image. Easier said than done! Haven't we all suffered endless put-downs in our own childhood? But let us comfort ourselves by the fact that we are clearly considerate and caring people who want the best for our children, otherwise we would not be reading this book. All of the affirmation activities are needed by us grown-ups just as much as the children, more so in some ways as we have probably had years of frustration and uncertainty already.

Ann Constanti

So we shall concentrate on enhancing everyone's self-concept: making people feel good about themselves. When we feel confident and valued for our own sake we can spare the energy to give our children the full love and attention they need. It is not always easy for us adults to pitch the right note in our relationships with children: we have to strike a balance between how far we guide them and how far we develop their own self-regulation; this will be an ever changing adaptation to their development and capabilities.

Our aim in the long run is that our children will be able to establish true independence of mind and spirit and become whole persons in their own right. The key to this approach may well be the nurturing of their creativity: their sense of music and poetry, rhythm and dance, literature and art. If we are only educated along intellectual lines, we miss out on the essential part of our personality which is concerned with feelings and emotions and therefore with love and security in our relationships. And to console the adults it is never too late to play and be creative just for the sake of it; this will bring us nearer to our true self and to our children whose saving grace is that they do play and create just for the sake of it. We shall be greatly helped in our relationships with children if we manage to do something creative with them: by playing together, dancing or making something new – a game, a toy? This is the best way of communicating and our relationships depend a great deal on communication. We generally think of communication as talk and we forget that the unspoken bonds of doing things together are a sort of inner communication.

There are also the non-verbal signs of the body language which can sometimes be much more expressive than mere words. But most important of all is the creative art of listening: we need to give children our full, undivided attention when we do listen and this often can ease some of the ever-lasting demands that parents and teachers are beset with. It is amusing that we spend the first years encouraging them to talk, delighting in every new word and phrase; yet as soon as they become as fluent as adults our one idea is to have some respite from the barrage of their questions and comments. We should at least treat them with as much respect and awareness as we hope we do with adults; but how often do we talk at, if not down to children instead of with them?

We are really talking about co-operation when we consider positive communication and it could be seen as the first principle of peaceful conflict-solving. The competitive element is easily detected in most talk, not merely the one-up-man-ship which can be a feature of modern life, but also the struggle to get the floor and make oneself heard. We are exposed to competition in every aspect of our lives; it pervades the home, the classroom and the media alike, and is frequently a source of stress, particularly with children who quickly see themselves as failures.

Yet it is co-operation that has always been an intrinsic part of human nature, as can be seen from the societies that have not yet been overwhelmed by the materialistic values of industrialisation. Here mutual co-operation is essential to everyday living, although all too often it is accompanied by abject poverty.

We can make conscious efforts to retrieve some of these co-operative values and we shall have a great headstart if we realise our own full potential. This is not to say that competition has no place at all: it can well be an addition like spice or salt to a main meal, but if it is the mainstay of any society this can be disastrous for adults and children alike.

The co-operative attitudes fostered by games and collaborative action can lessen the amount of conflicts in the everyday scene. There are also helpful techniques that can be learnt which give us opportunities of releasing the tension and coming to terms with the problems and conflicts that are bound to arise. If children start young with simplified patterns of conflict-solving, they will be more likely to try to arrive at agreed solutions, first guided by their adults and later on their own. These methods would be in contrast to the present general ethos, local or global, which sees the solution of any conflict in terms of a 'show down', usually with recourse to power and the threat of violence. We dare not risk that tomorrow's citizens perpetuate this attitude, otherwise there will be nothing else to perpetuate.

So let us face the future with optimism, with enhanced self-concepts, imaginative creativity, positive communication and co-operation and peaceful conflict-solving; in this way life can be much more fun and surely that is an aim worth achieving.

## A FEW PRACTICAL SUGGESTIONS ON HOW TO USE THIS BOOK

Parents and teachers can pick out the activities most suited to their needs and most of the ideas can be adapted for the home and the classroom. If there seem to be too few participants, most of the partner games can be played with just two people as a minimum; on the other hand larger numbers can be divided into small groups, if possible with a helper in each for the younger children.

Ideas more suited to the older age group are marked with a star, but we often under-estimate the capacity of young children, so if we make a progression starting with the simplest ideas, they can often surprise us with their ability to grasp more complicated activites. In the case of conflict-solving I have seen them progress from their usual appeal to the adults to administer justice to an attempt to talk it out on a one-at-a-time type of formula, which they have learnt to handle. On the question of age range there are virtually no limits with most of the suggestions in fact they often give a new lease of life to the grandparents and the elderly.

The chapters go in some sort of progression, so it is better to start with affirmation and creativity and some of the simplest communication skills. Of course co-operative games are always popular and there can be a gradation from the basic to the more complicated versions. A steady infusion is much better than a few intensive sessions as we are really concerned with a way of life; in this way these activities become a part of the family or classroom routine. A good idea is to pick out different exercises from each section to make variety; there will soon be special favourites and a demand for more.

Much can be learnt about co-operation by having a range of age levels like most families (some schools practise vertical grouping, where, for example, the 5's to 7 year olds are in the same class), here there can be a lot of give and take and also help given to the littler ones.

A word about the shy ones and there are many: they should never feel any pressure to join in and the rule about such devices as the Magic Shell, which is passed round in turn for children to have the right to speak, is that it is quite OK to pass and perhaps to take one's turn later on. Similarly with the practice of 'brainstorming': this is a process of receiving suggestions from everyone with no criticism of anyone's ideas, all are listed equally; then at a later stage there can be a choice made by the group as to which idea to follow.

Although many of the ideas have to be introduced by the adults, it is hoped that the children will take the initiative in directing the operation and inventing other activities of a similar nature.

## CHAPTER I        A POSITIVE SELF-CONCEPT

Positive Identity and Affirmation and Good Self-concept.
The Magic Circle.
Trust and Security.
Mutual Respect, Self-Reliance and Responsibility.
Feelings.
Appreciation of our Bodies.

# POSITIVE IDENTITY AND AFFIRMATION AND GOOD SELF-CONCEPT

Our confidence or lack of it usually dates from early childhood, although, of course, it is never too late to develop positive self-esteem. For most of us mortals we are very dependent on other people's opinions of us, and children are the most vulnerable in this position. Many of us emerge from childhood with a sense of personal failure, not least because the competitive society has inprinted us with our own inadequacy as compared with others. A sense of personal achievement and creativity for their own sakes are the remedies to enable us to face the 'free for all' modern world. This can only be gained by an independence from the opinions and successes of others and a firm conviction that we are all 'loveable and capable'.

## What We Can Do

**Silhouettes:** Life-size cut outs of children, stuck on wall, decorated with collages and affirming statements by the others.

**Shadow Silhouettes:** Child close to the wall against a large piece of art paper. A torch is shone on the profile or full-lenght and a third child draws round the outline. It is cut out and shaded in and then put up for "Guess who" and affirmed.

**Hand, Foot and finger Prints.** 'How I grow', traced round and cut out; then repeated some time later.

**Affirmation Notebook.** "All About Me", with pictures, photos, skills, etc.

**Tree of 'I Can',** labelled with each child's name hanging from a different branch and with leaves saying, eg. 'I can swim'. 'This year I can.... last year I couldn't. eg. skip or roller skate.

**Affirming Consequences:** everyone in a small circle puts their name at the bottom of a sheet of paper and passes it to the person on their right. He then writes something nice about her and folds it down at the top and passes it on to the next one. The sheets go round the circle each person writing something nice about the one whose name is on it and then folding it out of sight. When it comes back to the owner she has a whole lot of affirmations written about her. This can also be done with people saying nice things one after another about one chosen individual, with others taking their turn.

**And What Else are you Good at?:** In pairs one asks the other 'What are you good at?' and after their reply, 'What else are you good at?' and so on for three minutes.

**Three Wishes** for themselves and then three wishes for someone they love.

**Affirmation Cards:** Simple sentences written on cards with illustrations: eg. 'You have a nice smile'; 'You laugh a lot'. Every child in the group has one to give to somebody else.

**The IALAC Story:** this consists of wearing a badge labelled IALAC, which stands for 'I am lovable and capable'. It orginated from an idea of wearing a long strip of paper fastened to one's chest, and every time someone put you down you tore off a piece of the paper. It is often used as a story: say about a little girl who wears an IALAC paper which gets torn off progressively as she goes through the day, first at home and then at school. Of course one should have the sellotape ready to stick the pieces back on when someone is complimentary and appreciative. After a hard days 'being torn off a strip' the anti-dote is to repeat 'No matter what you do or say to me, I'm still a worthwile person'. Try it!

# THE MAGIC CIRCLE

From the very earliest traces of humanity we find that circles have played an exciting part both in physical and in spiritual life. Today we have few opportunities to sit in a circle in the warmth of a bonfire, but we can still feel the glow of friendship as we play circle games and share our feelings with one another in a ring. There really seems to be something magic about circles, whether they are sun, moon or down-to-earth with fairy mushroom rings! Certainly magic circle activities help to establish a secure self-image.

## What We Can Do

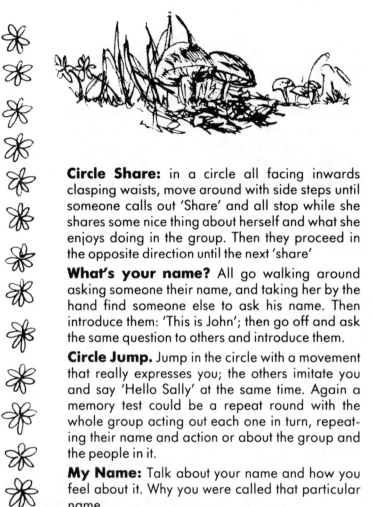

**Affirming Names:** Introducing yourself by name with an affirming description: 'Jolly Jane', 'Friendly Fred'. This can be a memory game, each introducing her neighbours on her right and left. Or each one can have a puppet to do this.

A variation of this is where the whole group repeats everyone's affirming name as a memory test after the first complete round; again puppets can be used.

**Sharing News:** Something I really like doing. Something I did that made me really happy.

Something I want to do this year. Draw a picture of it and discuss with partner.

If I could be an animal I would be a _____ _____ because _____

**Making you Laugh:** Round a circle the first one starts by trying to make the next one smile or laugh. The standard reply has to be, 'I love you but I just can't smile.' Words and gestures to make him smile or laugh are allowed, but no touching or tickling!

**Circle Share:** in a circle all facing inwards clasping waists, move around with side steps until someone calls out 'Share' and all stop while she shares some nice thing about herself and what she enjoys doing in the group. Then they proceed in the opposite direction until the next 'share'

**What's your name?** All go walking around asking someone their name, and taking her by the hand find someone else to ask his name. Then introduce them: 'This is John'; then go off and ask the same question to others and introduce them.

**Circle Jump.** Jump in the circle with a movement that really expresses you; the others imitate you and say 'Hello Sally' at the same time. Again a memory test could be a repeat round with the whole group acting out each one in turn, repeating their name and action or about the group and the people in it.

**My Name:** Talk about your name and how you feel about it. Why you were called that particular name.

# TRUST AND SECURITY

Trust is a basic human quality and it can be nourished from the day the baby is born. Throughout early childhood trust is built up through personal relationships; there must be enough security to approach new experiences with openness and confidence and at the same time a realistic mistrust of dangerous situations, whether physical or personal.

Trust exercises can enhance our natural feelings of faith in our fellow human beings and help build up caring feelings towards others whilst being able to rely and depend on them. Erik Erikson says that the right balance between trust and mistrust is the very first stage of a young child's development.

## What We Can Do

**Partners Blind Trust:** One leading the blind-folded person protecting him from all obstacles; at first with your arm around him, then hands clasped, and finally, after some practice, guiding with finger tips.

**Trust Instructions,** blindfold: guiding by talking, e.g. 'Go forward', 'Stop', 'Take two paces to the left'. Take turns in pairs.

**Guide Dog:** Pretend to be the guide dog for the blind.

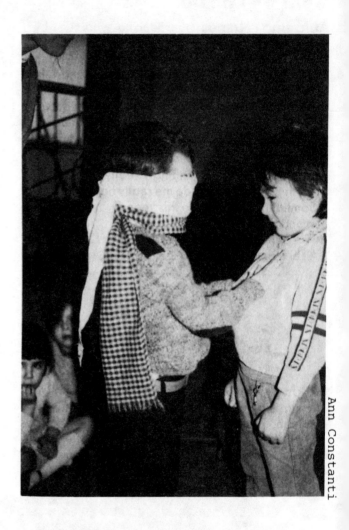

Ann Constanti

**\* Swaying in the breeze:** Take turns to stand in a **small** closely knit circle and sway with upright body, letting yourself go, knowing that the circle will not let you fall. This can also be done with a partner, when great care must be taken to support the trusting one and be strong enough not to let him fall.

**\* Helter Skelter:** A double row of players facing each other and clasping both hands of the person opposite to make a firm base. In turns, each child goes down the line head first on her tummy, supported by the arms and gently eased over the 'hills' as the group wave their arms up and down.

# MUTUAL RESPECT, SELF-RELIANCE AND RESPONSIBILTIES

Mutual respect is the whole basis for getting on with people and this applies particularly to respect between the generations, parents and children, teachers and pupils. It is very easy for adults to feel superior to children; after all it is natural, grown-ups have so much more experience! But children have the spontaneity and enthusiasm that we have so often lost, so our exchanges should be mutually beneficial. How often do we tell children what they should think and how they should act and how often do we correct them rather than let them explore their own feelings or learn acceptable behaviour from us as models and from experience? This mutual respect does not mean that overall rules of conduct and responsibilities are not laid down and agreed, and, we hope, acted upon!

## What We Can Do

**The Responsibility Wheel:** Jobs can be volunteered for and allocated on a rota basis with adults and children all participating.

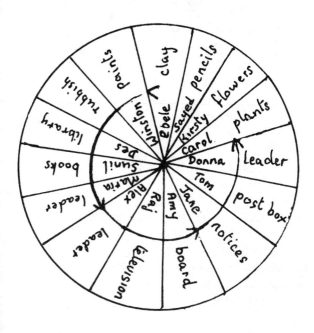

**Conch Shell:** Anyone who holds the shell (or the magic microphone) has the right to speak and no one else. The group can decide how it is allocated so that everyone takes turns and that those who do not want to speak are also respected when they 'pass'. This freedom from pressure often gives them the confidence to speak later on. Many of the games in this book can be directed by the children and there are also opportunities for individuals to take over, even temporarily. Children should be encouraged to make up their own variations and ideas for games; once given the confidence they have lots of imaginative ideas.

★ **Put Ups:** Think about a person who put you up and made you feel really somebody, made you happy with yourself. Draw a picture showing an example of this.

**Put Ups and Put Downs:** The same as above and then another picture showing just the opposite: someone who made you feel really insignificant and stupid. This exercise can be very revealing to adults when they do it; it can take us back to our childhood and often give us greater understanding of what children are feeling.

# FEELINGS

In Britain we have been socialised to keep our feelings to ourselves, especially boys and men. We are now gradually becoming aware of our needs to acknowledge our emotions in order to be complete human beings. From a very early age our feelings should be able to be expressed openly (babies usually have no difficulty here!) We need to show our children that it is natural to express strong feelings, not only of love and tenderness, but also of anger and hatred, and when they are more open we can try to deal with them instead of repressing them.

## What We Can Do

**Happy–Sad:** We can pass our hand over our face while we switch expressions (rather like peek-a-boo).

**Pass the Mask:** In a circle one starts by making a face expressing an emotion: sorrow, disappointment, surprise, etc. and passes it on to the next one who imitates it.

**Change the Mask:** This time after imitating, she wipes her face clean and does another expression for her neighbour, and so on round the circle.

**Happy-Sad Sculptures:** In pairs take turns in 'moulding' a real human sculpture – your partner! The others guess how they are feeling. Groups can also make tableaux of real people depicting a particular emotion: eg. grief, excitement, anger.

**\*Happy Memories:** share in a circle your good (and bad!) memories: e.g. a time when I was scared.

**\*Left Out:** 3 people indulge in nonsense talk: 'gobbledegook'. Then 2 concentrate on each other and leave the other one out of it. In turns, how does it feel to be left out and isolated, even for a minute?

**\*Let me in!** In a tight circle of people, shoulder to shoulder, one person is outside and tries to get in. If she succeeds the one who let her in goes out. How does it feel?

# APPRECIATION OF OUR BODIES

We are finally emerging from the sense of shame of our bodies that permeated so much of Victorian Britain and was conveyed to so many parts of the world by the missionaries. The attitudes of our elders about how we view our bodies influence us from birth and a healthy appreciation of the body and all it does for us can be built up from a very early age. This appreciation underlies many of the games and activities that are described in this book; there is much shaping, touching and hugging of our bodies and this helps us to become more aware of the completeness of our body, mind and soul.

## What we can do:

**Relaxation:** is really enjoyed by young children, starting with tensing up the toes and then wriggling them and so on, working up the whole body in this way.

**Massage:** is a wonderful relaxer: foot and body massage can be done by a partner, and group massage in a circle with everyone massaging the neck and back of the person in front of them, sitting on the floor or standing.

**Deep breathing:** is also a perfect relaxer, before and after any of the activities in this book.

**Body Jigsaw:** one child lies on the floor and the others join him and fit themselves into a big human jigsaw, with their bodies bent or stretched out to make a solid mass. Then they all get up and run around and then try to put themselves back in exactly the same position as before so that they remake the 'jigsaw'.

**Variation:** make a machine of bodies or a terrifying monster. This will need a good deal of co-operation.

**Body Letters:** combining by making their bodies into shapes to make letters, and then words and even postcards.

## CHAPTER II    CREATIVITY

Fantasy and Imagination
Art
Music and Poetry
Dance and Movement
Love of Nature
Spiritual Values

# FANTASY AND IMAGINATION

All small children have great flights of fancy; in fact in the early years it is difficult for them to know what is imagination and what is reality. In the progress of distinguishing between the two it is the flow of fantasy that can be lost for ever, particularly if their confusion is disparaged or ridiculed. We need to foster their creative imagination so that they are able to function at both levels and also combine the two.

## What we can do:

**Guided Fantasy:** can release us from the mundane realities of life and take us whereever we will. Children love a guided fantasy: for example, 'Dream Flight': it would be to the moon, the planets and the stars, or over the seas in a magic boat, or at the bottom of the ocean: reality in nature can mingle freely with the world of dreams and imagery. Generally the adult takes the initiative and tells the fantasy and the children can have their eyes closed or they can gaze at lighted candles or a crystal ball.

**Stories:** which can be acted out or mimed. Afterwards, can be first read or told as a guided fantasy.

**Dream Flight:** this is a delightful story by Caroline Askar about children watching the caterpillars, who then turn into chrysalises and finally emerge as bright butterflies who fly high into the sky. The children want to fly too, but although they jump in the air and flap their arms it is no use! Then a large butterfly comes and tells them a special and true secret: that children can fly anywhere they choose, just by closing their eyes and using their minds and imagining they are soaring high, high above the green hills, skimming above the waves, or gliding over the rooftops of the town and talking to the pigeons!

**Mind Pictures:** Shut your eyes for a little while and then paint what you have seen.

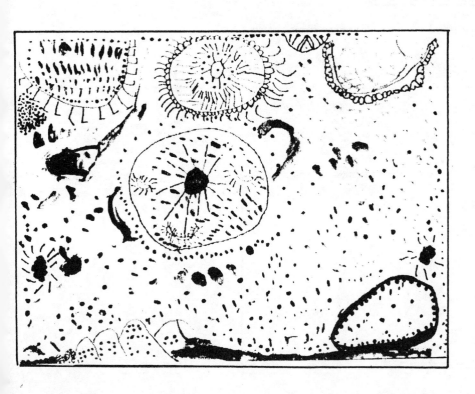

# ART

Art is one of the main sources of self-expression for the very young: their arranging of pebbles and shells, their brush strokes of vivid colour are performed with full concentration and unselfconscious effort. This original spontaneity can so easily be crushed by well-meaning adults who want to help them to get perspective or teach them accuracy in drawing. Let them produce their creations without interference – it is part of their innermost world that they are portraying.

   Jon Maddison, a follower of Arno Stern, the founder of Expression Painting, writes, 'Most of us are taught from an early age that painting is a skill, a very specialised art form that requires dedication, training and an inherent thing called talent. Painting is thus made into something which is inaccessible to most people, something that at best we are able only to look at, not create. A whole visual language is cut off from us, so that years later we find ourselves saying things like, "I have never been able to paint".... Yet within each of us there is a seldom-tapped well of expression that can be released through painting in circumstances where our learned expectations of the painting process can be abandoned' (Expression painting. A Creative Learning Process).

   Although many games call upon the illustrative abilities of children, these should not be confused with pure art sessions where there is complete freedom of expression and everything is freely available in the way of paints, paper, clay and collage materials where the atmosphere is tranquil and compltely non-judgmental on the part of the adults.

## A child's expression painting.

# MUSIC AND POETRY

In many societies music is the heart-beat of life; in many African societies for example it would be inconceivable to lead a life where music played a minor role; it is part of the essence of their existence. In the same way there are societies where almost everyone can express themselves in poetry as well as prose; these characteristics are rooted in their deepest traditions and are in no way the monopoly of the elite or the wealthy.

All children have a natural sense of rhythm and they delight in making music and singing, and if gently encouraged are able to express themselves in words with creative spontaneity. Too many adults have been discouraged in their early explorations of tone and voice and poetry; these are very delicate personal experiences which need to be respected. I have known grown-ups who have never sung a note since they were turned out of the singing class for being 'growlers'! Fortunately it is never too late to regain the confidence needed to make music and poetry, but it is so much better to ensure that it never happens to our children when they are young.

Alfred Nieman, the composer, puts this point beautifully in an article entitled, 'The Courage to Improvise Music': 'I put forth the idea that children should not be *taught* music, they should be encouraged to *make* music..... The teachers should be the catalyst, working to release the children's energies, to give them ideas, to provide instruments so they can make music to give their own story and ideas a picture, an image. Children are marvellous at that sort of thing. You play a loud sound and ask them what that sound feels like. *Ask them;* it's surprising the things they will say or imagine about a loud sound. Then you play a little 'plunk' at the top of the piano – what's that sound like? One will say a bird, one will say it's a little cloud or a drop of water.' Now let's assume the children have got some percussion instruments, then say, 'All right, let's make some music with loud and soft noises'. They share, and it is amazing the things they do. They begin to make *form;* it comes out of them naturally. The children have form inside them and it is written large'. (in 'Educare', Nov-march 1986).

## What We Can Do

**Guess the instruments:** What instruments do you hear? e.g the drum, the tambourine, the piano. What was the order in which they were played?

**Animal sounds:** Using one's voice to imitate animal sounds. Guess who is doing it. (eyes closed).

**Conducting the orchestra:**
Play a definite rhythm with everyone having a percussion instrument. Taking turns with conducting eg. slow/quick, or loud/soft with the baton being lowered further and further down to get softer until it touches the floor for 'stop'.

**Thunderstorm.** in a *small* circle the leader passes round rapidly the sound of her two hands being rubbed together, and everyone does this in turn; this is for rain. Then clicking of the fingers all the way round for hail, then stamping of the feet for thunder and finally back to the clicks, getting slower and slower and then only the hand rubbing until the storm is over.

**Circle Clap:** Clapping rhythm passed round the circle; Variations: two going round in opposite directions. These can be taped to see if the rhythm is maintained.

**Musical Characters:** With a simple instrument or the piano give an improvisation of different animals: eg. a mouse, an elephant, a deer. Can you extend this to your family or your school mates? You need no expertise in playing the instrument, rather an intuitive feeling that you can express in notes and rhythm.

**My Bonnie:** When singing this favourite song, bob up and down everytime a word begins with the letter 'B'. eg. go down for the first 'B' as in Bonnie, then up again for the next Bonnie and so on.

**Rounds** are fun to sing and to conduct and they give a good feeling of community. New ones could be invented on the lines of 'London's Burning' for example.

**Humming Bees:** Choose several well-known songs or nursery rhymes. Give a picture secretly or whisper to each one what their tune is. They then go round humming it to find others with the same tune. Then they can sing it all together! The same game can be played with the vowels AEIOU, finishing up with a grand finale with a conductor going loud/soft, etc.

**Singing Together:** This gives a great sense of unity and there are many song books which give a variety of themes which would be in complete harmony with the activities in this book.

# LOVE OF NATURE

All children have an intrinsic love of nature and now that so many live in a crowded inner-city environment, we need to make special efforts to nourish and succour this wondrous gift. In the same way we can foster and care for all sorts of wildlife and plants, even in the concrete jungle. Many human beings have become alienated from nature, in fact the only experience some children have of it is on television; this may be an inadequate substitute, but it is worth while encouraging them to watch the nature programmes and to talk about them afterwards. It is all too true that some children think that milk comes from the supermarket and that there really are spaghetti trees! We need to put our children in touch with real nature once more and in doing so we can plant seeds of fulfillment which can last for the rest of their lives.

## What We Can Do

**My Tree to Hug:** In pairs one is blindfold and the other leads her to her special tree in a roundabout way, noting some clues in passing. She can touch and hug the tree before being led back along a different trail. Now she has to find her tree with her eyes open and with the support of her guide. This works well with one adult and one child.

**Nature Trail:** in small groups visit various sites, which have been prepared in advance with a helper waiting to explain the task. At each site perform some activity; eg. crawl blindfold along a log; help to make a log cabin; design a nature collage on a board. It should be organised so that there is only one group at a time at each site.

**Group Treasure Hunt:** similar to the nature trail, but at each site there would be a hidden clue to get to the next site. As soon as anyone finds the clue he shares it with the whole group and they proceed all together to the next site to find the clue. The Treasure would be something that could easily be shared, eg. a hidden apple or orange, one for everyone.

**Nature Night Walk:** with torches, led by someone who knows the way and can identify night birds and creatures. This is always exciting for children.

**Lie Back and Enjoy Nature:** Lie on your back and look up through the branches of a tree, or in the long grass at the side of a meadow, or on the borders of a stream. Stay listening for five to ten minutes. This could also be an eyes closed experience. If real nature is not available then a guided fantasy with taped sounds might be the next best thing.

A FLOWER WITH LITE

**Nature Walk:** collecting all sort of specimens of interest: grasses, stones, mosses, and certain flowers that you are allowed to pick — just one of each. You could also look at the collection, and then cover it up and try to recall all that was there. Take away something, what is missing?

# SPIRITUAL VALUES

There are now many instances of young children meditating at home or in school. To most Westerners this seems alien to their culture, yet it is not so far removed from all of the other creative experiences we have described in that it reaches down to the inner self from where much of our creative inspiration flows.

The meditation or relaxation can be a guided fantasy or concentration on one concept such as joy. Children can close their eyes and enter into their inner minds, putting away the many thoughts that assail all of us all of the time. The atmosphere is peaceful with some music to begin with and perhaps lighted candles; then an adult could begin to guide them in deep breathing; they could breathe in lovely feelings of peace and happiness and breathe out all the nasty thoughts. Gradually they are full of joy and happiness, they are overflowing with it so that they can spare some for someone else, someone sitting near them. With still more they can give it to all the family or all the class, then to the people living near them or the whole school, then extending to the village or town, to the whole country, the whole world, and finally the universe with its myriads of suns!

What has been amazing is that after this five to ten minute concentration they do some art which can produce extraordinary results unlike anything they have ever done before; the pictures have a radiance and beauty which reflect something that has taken place within them.

**Example of children's paintings after meditation.**

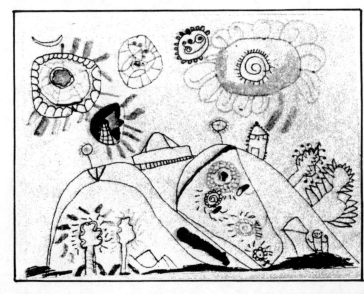

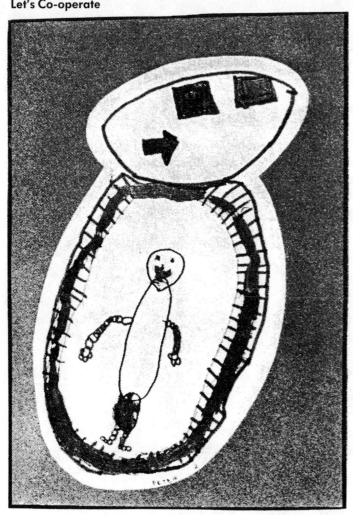

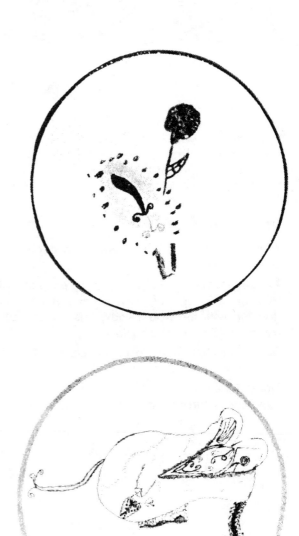

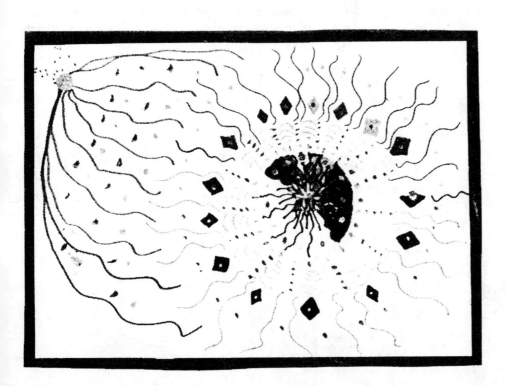

# DANCE AND MOVEMENT

It is a wonderful sight to see young children moving and dancing spontaneously to music; they are unaware of any audience, carried away in a world of their own. The old song recorded from the Appalachian mountains expresses this feeling: 'Dance, dance, wherever you may be; for I am the Lord of the Dance said he'. In many countries music and rhythm are such an integral part of their society that life would be meaningless without it.

## What We Can Do

Dance spontaneously to music, individually, then couples, threes, etc.

**Finger Dancing:** In twos, guiding each other by touching the tips of each other's fingers and dancing with the whole body; this gives a lot of freedom with sensitive contact.

**Shadow Dancing:** following close behind the partner and mirroring their dance.

**Back to Back Dancing:** feeling the partner's movements, through the spine and legs.

**Circle Dances:** All countries have circle dances and it is good to learn all sorts: eg. from India, Greece, Mexico, etc. Sacred dances are becoming popular: a favourite where we sing to our partners:
'To you I give,
From you I receive
Together we share,
In this we live.' with appropriate actions. Then we move in opposite directions to greet the next partner in the same way, and so on round the circle.

**Tai 'Chi Chuan:** A wonderfully relaxed form of movement which originates from China. it is a combination of harmonious movement and a form of meditation, and is becoming widespread in the West.

CHAPTER III

## COMMUNICATION

Awareness and Observation
Non-Verbal Communication
Creative Writing
Story Telling
Creative Listening
Drama
Discussion and Decision Making
The Media

# AWARENESS AND OBSERVATION

Most young children are disconcertingly aware of everything that is going on and we should nurture these powers rather than hush them up! Awareness of other people and their feelings is the basis of peaceful co-existence in the future. This seems a long haul from the minute observational powers of young infants and their almost uncanny detecting of moods and emotions around them.

## What We Can Do

**Kim's Game:** is a perennial favourite: small objects on a tray which are covered from sight after one minute and then as many as possible are recalled.

**What Have I Changed?:** Someone changes 3 or more things about him/herself and the partner spots them.

**Sensing the Senses:** seeing, hearing, touching, tasting and smelling can be extended with fun: guessing different sights and sounds, textures, tastes and smells, eg. feely bags, photos, tapes, musical instruments, etc.

**Group Shift:** Spotting the order in which 6 people line up, spotting any change; recalling their particular order. A variation would be for each of the six to choose a different positon and another group of six tries to reproduce the whole line from memory.

**Partner Statues:** in pairs, one takes up a particular position and the other who is blindfold tries to imitate it through feeling. Take turns.

**Awareness of the Handicapped.** Many of these exercises can be directed towards an awareness of being deprived of one or more of the senses. The blindfold games are particularly striking, but also ears can be blocked up with wax and the experience of deafness can be felt. There could be a progression to awareness of any disability: "What would I feel like if I had it?"

**Magic Mind Reading.** A small group sits in a circle and concentrates with eyes closed on one person in the group. After a minute or so they write the first letter of her name on a piece of paper, or whisper to the adult. Sometimes it works, or at least for some children!

**Variation.** The small group chooses three or four objects and in a circle each one chooses one and concentrates on it. Then as above.

**Know Your Potato:** Have a heap of potatoes of similar size and get each child to choose one. They look at it for a minute and then the potatoes are put into the heap again. Can you find your own potato? This can be done with oranges, apples, conkers, etc.

# NON-VERBAL COMMUNICATION

Often what we say is not as relevant as how we say it, whether it is in tone of voice, facial expression or body movements. Children are quick to interpret the real message and when there seems to them to be a contradiction they feel confused and begin to lose trust in what the adults say. We seldom talk about these hidden messages and bring them out into the open; if we did, this should clear the air and help us all to try to be consistent in our communication.

## What we can do:

**Circle Squeeze** or **Telegraph:** Clasping hands in a circle send a message of sqeezes round, eg. two long squeezes and three little ones. Later have two messages going in different directions. This can also be played with winks and nudges!

**Follow the Sound:** one makes the sound and it goes round the circle: add another sound going round in the opposite direction. Children can take it in turns to make up the sound, eg. animal noises, nature sounds, machines and vehicles.

**Are You Happy or Sad?:** In turns make your expression the opposite of what you say you feel. eg. 'I am very happy!', yet the tears are running down your face!

**Nonsense Talk or Gobbledegook:** in pairs try to understand what the other is getting at; discuss aftewards. Portray mood changes, angry, loving, sad, etc. and tell how you felt.

**Funny Foot:** One starts off round the circle saying, 'This is my foot', but he points to his elbow. The next one can say, 'This is my elbow, but she points to her ear. A simpler version is not to follow on with the last part of the body that was mentioned, eg. the elbow; it can be any part. Sooner or later they forget about it having to be the wrong part!

# CREATIVE WRITING

Can we express ourselves in writing with some of the spontaneity of speech? It is more difficult and perhaps we set young children too ambitious a task when we expect them to write long accounts. Their writing skills are only gradually developing, and their inspiration can be lost in the sheer mechanical effort of forming the letters. Sympathetic adults can help by writing what children want to say, with encouragement to write a title; making their own book in this way will be a stage in their progression towards doing it all by themselves. Illustrations and photographs can enhance the booklet, and it will be something that will build up their self-confidence, especially if they do the illustrations and take the photographs themselves.

Many children get the message from adults and their peers that a bought greetings card is better than their own efforts; of course it has been designed by a professional and should not be compared to a child's creative effort. We should encourage them to do their own with little loving messages or a tiny poem and show them how much they are appreciated; it will be a great boost to their morale. Poems are not something to be afraid of if they are approached from the earliest years: reading and enjoying them is a step towards writing them, just two lines that do not rhyme to begin with, then on to simple structures such as the Japanese haiku. A *Letter Box* in the home or the classroom is a great way of promoting creativity in writing and also making a more loving atmosphere; it can be used for celebrations or all sorts: birthdays, Valentines, Christmas, Diwali, Eid and as Humpty Dumpty said, one can have un-birthday cards and greetings too.

# STORY TELLING

In all societies the elders have recounted stories to the children: folk tales, myths and accounts of great deeds of the past, and these played a great part in teaching about the culture. Today in the 'West' we have a wondrous selection of children's books that are beautifully illustrated and freely available from children's libraries; but welcome as they are, they cannot compensate for the tradition of story telling. As a child my favourite request was 'Tell me a story about when you were little'; and there seems to be a deep desire on the part of children to know more about their immediate past and how it has changed. It needs a great effort on our part to tell and not read the story, but the appreciation is worth the effort. We can all manage 'The Three Bears' and that's often about all, except the nursery rhymes which, like the traditional stories handed down, were learnt on our parents' laps.

## What we can do

**Group Story.** Each one in the circle giving one word to made up a story. Later each one giving a little sentence, always with the option of 'passing'. An imaginary book can be passed round.

**Story Bag:** have a bag full of toys which can be passed round as the next inspiration for the story, with each child taking one out as for a lucky dip.

**Nursery Rhyme Stories:** Tell simple stories about nursery rhymes or folk tales: eg. Jack and Jill or Jack and the Beanstalk.

# CREATIVE LISTENING

How many of us experience real active listening? We are generally half listening and already formulating in our minds what we are going to say next; and it is true that if we don't, someone else will break in and the opportunity to express one's own ideas is lost. With children we listen even less and we interrupt them even more than we do adults. This information came out in a recent study which went on to say that we interrupt girls twice as much as we do boys!

With creative listening we give our undivided attention and forgo the temptation to give advice at the end. Children are swamped by directives and suggestions from adults; they rarely have the freedom to be quite frank and open with the assurance that they will not be judged for it in any way.

## What we can do:

**Whispers:** Whispering a sentence round in a circle and see what it turns out like when it has done the round. (The message reputedly sent in the 1914-18 war, 'We are going to advance, please send reinforcements', came out the other end as 'We are going to a dance, please send three and four-pence', which is just another example of how easily in war time there can be a disregard for the safety of the forces who are ordered into battle)

**Listening to your partner:** As part of the circle affirmation games, 'What is your favourite etc?' Listen *without* interrupting, then report on what your partner said.

Similarly with introductions and itnerviews, the reporter does not interrupt until the statement is finished.

**Sophie Says:** This is an adaptation of the game, 'Simon Says', where the leader gives various commands, but if he does not precede the instruction with 'Simon Says' the children must not do it and if they do they are out! In 'Sophie Says' they are not out, they just start making a circle inside the original one and in the end everyone is in the inner circle.

**Directions:** Listen to directions and then follow them exactly: eg. take one pace forward, turn to your right, two bunny jumps forward, etc.

**Silence:** listen with eyes closed to see if there are any sounds when we try to be completely silent. Discuss what we have heard and in what order.

**Draw a Picture:** one describes a picture and the other(s) draw it without being able to see it. Discuss how difficult it was.

**Music Listening:** Which instrument did you hear? a drum, a tambourine, or cymbals?

# DISCUSSION AND DECISION MAKING

Discussion and decision making are often considered only suitable for older children, (although this is usually lip service only); younger ones are thought to be too immature for such democratic procedures. We all know that children match up to whatever expectations we may have of them; so, if we give them the chance to discuss and produce solutions, they will come up with a lot of sense. The opportunity of choosing has to be a way of life from early childhood and this will be a sheet anchor for decision making later on; of course the choices should be within the realms of possibility and have due consideration for others.

## What we can do:

Small group discussions on everyday issues: which programme we are going to watch? which games to play? These kinds of decisions are made anyhow in the rough and tumble of getting on with each other. The adults' delicate role is governed by how far there should be any structure. Perhaps this should be used only when the children appeal for some kind of arbitration; they could then be guided into listening to each one's point of view and then reaching a joint decision. All of the other activities, the affirmation and the conflict-solving will pave the way for a more spontaneous approach and children's sense of fairness can be nurtured in this context.

It is worth mentioning that participants should feel free to be able to disagree; so often it is not a question of right and wrong, it is often the case that people see things differently. Children (like so many adults!) tend to think in terms of opposites and the experience of many different points of view is vital to their understanding.

**Spin the Bottle:** This is an example of a class decision of how to solve the problem of the clamouring every time someone has to be chosen.

# DRAMA

Drama is one of the best ways of promoting empathy and understanding towards other people. We should aim at preserving young children's natural propensity towards play acting and fantasy and thus enable them to imagine themselves in someone else's shoes. Drama is a co-operative activity by its very nature and a great deal of give and take is learnt in the planning, rehearsing and performing stages. An audience is not necessary, as the sense of fulfillment in working together is highly rewarding for its own sake. Mime is especially suitable for young children, they can concentrate on the feelings and expressions without having to worry about the words.

## What we can do

**Magic Box.** an imaginary object taken out of a gaily decorated box. Each child has a turn at miming it with some action. Simple examples should be given, eg. an orange being peeled. Guess what it is.

**Mime Objects:** miming with a real object, eg. an umbrella; it can be a horse or a hockey stick; children guess.

**Mime a Job or a Game:** eg, a fisherman or a game of tennis.

**Mime an Incident:** eg. a boat trip in a storm, or rescuing someone who has fallen through the ice on the pond.

**Group Mimes:** catching the train, street market, seaside, shop, snack bar, dentists, hairdresser, playground. Planning in the group beforehand *or* spontaneous improvisations.

**Mime 'Talk':** children mouth the words but do not speak; this can be used in all of the miming ideas, eg. 'Give Me a Banana'.

**Challenge Mimes:** Mime something really difficult to do; eg. carry two ice cream cornets across a sweltering hot beach; learning to roller skate for the first time.

**Puppets** can be used for any of the drama activities, as well as the circle activities.

**Family of Puppets:** each puppet taking a role in the family with everyday activities or special occasions like a wedding or a festival or a picnic. We could watch out for gender stereotyping here!

**Circle Puppets:** Any of the circle games described in this book with the owners of the puppets speaking for them. We could include negative ideas: 'the naughtiest thing I have ever done'; or 'I hate laying the table'; or 'I hate cleaning out my hamster'. Other puppets worked by children could take the adult role to reply to the last two.

It is worth paying a lot of attention to drama and building it up through mime and puppets; it will also play an important part in peaceful conflict-solving techniques.

## What we can do

**Story Drama**: Simple acting out of well-known stories: The Three Bears, Cinderella, folk tales of different countries, eg. Anansi stories.

**Group Drama:** themes where the powerless children are given the control: the shy or the younger ones. eg. hospital ward and they are the doctors or matrons: a burglar scene where they are the detectives; the warders in a prison. See page on 'Empowerment'.

**Bran-Tub Lucky Dips:** In small groups, a bag containing various toys or things is given to each group. Make up a group story about them. eg. fire engine, baby, horse, fireman.

**Group Themes 'Let me in, Let me out'** : This needs a lot of preliminary discussion about feelings; eg. 'Let me in' on a game in the playground, or coming to school for the first time. 'Let me out' in a crowd of adults Christmas shopping, or shut up in a lavatory. Fears are voiced and acted out which are shared by everyone, but often it is difficult to admit one's own inadequacies.

**Desert Island Drama:** Draw a large island on paper and each child adds something, then make up a story around it and act out. It might be an island of monsters, giants, pirates, space people on a planet. A stranger can be introduced, will they accept him? What is he or she like? What must the stranger feel like?

**Drama Sheet:** A very large sheet can be thrown over various obstacles, it can represent a snow scene or a desert; the children can tunnel, go in caves, climb mountains etc., make up a story with adventures in strange land, again meeting strange people.

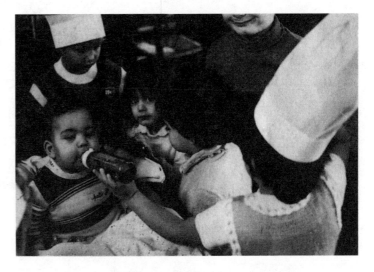

# THE MEDIA

For young children television is by far the greatest influence from the media; many of them in the 'West' spend as many hours watching television as they attend school! It is easier said than done to restrict viewing, but it is really necessary if they are to grow up as active participants in society. We can help by discussing the programmes, viewing together and talking about them afterwards, and also providing creative alternatives. A good rule for families is to make meals 'television free', as these times can be the only ones when there is a sharing of conversation between everyone. This also should entail sharing the chores instead of the children viewing and the adults doing all the housework. The ability to see through the sensationalism and the endless diet of violence is something we can aim at; and this includes teachers in the classroom who can made a point of helping their pupils to be critical and discriminating viewers. Then of course peaceful conflict-solving comes into the picture with different members of the family wanting different programmes; in fact television is often a big source of dispute and everyone needs to know exactly what the rules are.

## What we can do:

★ **Video Making:** Making our own or 'pretend' video. 'Pretend' would be pictures on a long strip of wallpaper.

★ **Real Video** would be for older children. Many of the activities in this book would be suitable film material: Co-operative Games, Our Play etc. The younger age group could be filmed doing these activities, by the adults at first and then the older ones.

★ **'Radio Station':** giving local news, again the older group possibly interviewing the younger ones as well as their peers and adults.

**Choosing the Programmes:** making the choice of viewing a really democratic procedure and sticking to it. This can be a routine instead of just slumping down to watch the box. In this way individuals' choice can be respected.

**Watch and Say What You Think.** Choose certain programmes and talk about them afterwards in the classroom or at home.

**CHAPTER IV**  **CO-OPERATION**
Co-operative Games
Doing Things Together
Life-Affirming Toys

# CO-OPERATIVE GAMES

In this book the games suggested are all supportive and non-competitive; they are sociable in that they have a wonderful capacity to make people feel connected, and having a sense of belonging in the group. So many of the games played today are highly competitive where the great majority of the participants fail; and in the long run this takes away a lot of the sheer fun, however 'sporting' they may be. Co-operative games can be played with just two people (or even one co-operating with himself!) or almost any number. They can be played in the home and the classroom, or out of doors in gardens, parks, fields or playgrounds. Rules are made to be modified and the great idea is to make up one's own original activities. It is interesting to note that children's games, handed down through generations of children are usually very supportive and accepting of everyone who joins in; this is brought out clearly in the books of the Opies on the lore of children. There are wonderful books on co-operative games now being published in America, Canada, Great Britain and other countries, and these hve been a great source of stimulation and inspiration. Their help is fully acknowledged with grateful thanks and they are fully listed as highly recommended in the Resources section.

## What we can do:

**Partners Co-operating.** In the Playfair movement (see resources), there is great emphasis on finding alternative ways of choosing partners so that no one feels unchosen or left out. These ideas are co-operative in themselves and develop a sense of belonging; eg. choose someone of the same height as you are, born in the same month, day or year; someone wearing a colour that you are wearing.

**Partner Jigsaw.** Find the one who has the other part of your postcard jigsaw.

**Mirroring.** Facing your partner and doing exactly the same things; in the end no one is leading and there can be perfect synchronism. This can also be done with puppets and also as a group, either with partners facing each other in two long rows or the whole group mirroring one person or in fours with two couples mirroring each other.

**Musical Laps:** there can be several versions based on musical chairs: one is when the chairs are taken away as usual, but when the music stops everyone has either to sit on a chair or cushion or someone's lap until at last there is one chair and everyone is 'sitting' on the lap of the person on it. It is best to have a rule that they sit with legs outstretched if it would be too heavy or uncomfortable for some children. Another version is

**Musical Squat:** when the music stops the whole circle sits on the lap of the person behind them; this is done by clasping the waist of the person in front and gently lowering oneself on to the lap of the person behind. If the circle does not collapse then everyone has won!

Ann Constanti

**Partner Pull Up:** In twos pull yourselves up from a sitting position and then from back to back.

Ann Constanti

**Animal Partners:** each one has a slip of paper with the name of an animal, two for each animal, and either by miming or making the noise of the animal they find their counterpart.

## Activities for a number of children:

**Cross the Bay:** A giant crab who only walks sideways is waiting to catch you as you all cross they bay; if you get caught you too become a giant crab ready to catch anyone crossing. This can be played as separate crabs or an enormous one all joining up together and walking sideways. This is sometimes played with children crossing the river where the crocodile lies in wait.

**Logs or Crocodiles:** Another crocodile game is where half the children are logs and half people swimming across the river. The 'logs' are secretly told that they are really crocodiles, so when a swimmer holds on to one of them it gobbles her up and two of them become one big crocodile log to lie in wait for the next victim.

**Catch the Snake's Tail:** four, five or even six children in a row clasping the waist of the one in front of them. The chaser tries to catch hold of the snake's tail and the snake tries to escape; if the chaser succeeds she becomes the tail and the 'head' becomes the chaser. This can also be played in groups of three who are camels: the head, the body and tail.

**Blind Man's Bluff:** in a *safe* restricted area. As anyone gets tagged they are also blindfolded and work together in pairs, then 3's and so on until the last one is caught.

## Variations on Tag:

**Scarecrow** where the catcher has arms outstretched while everyone has to cross the field; when tagged they form two scarecrows with open arms.

**Ball of Wool or String:** take a ball of thick wool and give it to each one in turn; they wind it round themselves in an imaginative way and pass it on to the next; when all are attached, unravel.

# CO-OPERATIVE CIRCLE GAMES

Many well-known games have a disadvantage in that they eliminate the players one by one so that slower children often spend most of the time watching the more successful ones. We can easily adapt these games to situations where no one loses and everyone gains; often these are more hilarious than the original ones. All of the books on co-operative games make this fundamental principle.

**General Post:** A favourite of long standing is the circle game where everyone has the name of a town or a fruit and the one in the middle calls out an exchange, 'London to Paris' or 'Banana to Orange', which little ones find easier. As they change places the middle one tries to get an empty place and the one left out takes a turn in the middle. When 'General Post' is called out, or 'Fruit Basket' everyone changes. More than two towns or fruit can be called out at te same time for those children to change their places.

**Musical Hoops:** When the music stops you get into a hoop which is lying on the ground; with the gradual removal of the hoops, one at a time, the end is where they are all crowding into the last hoop.

**Untwist:** In a circle close eyes and grasp any other hands. Open your eyes and try to unravel the group without losing complete hand contact.

**Car Race:** the first one in the circle shouts 'Zoom', which is picked up quickly by the next one and so on round the circle. If anyone calls out 'Eek', the 'car' has to brake and go in the opposite direction. Each one only has one turn in calling 'Eek'. A progression is when there are two zooms going round in opposite directions with 'Eeks' sending them off in the other direction.

★ **Elephant and Palm Tree:** This is an old favourite. In threes we rehearse **Elephant:** with the middle person bending down with straight arms in front of her for the trunk and the two people at either side of her become ears with their outside arms held akimbo. **Palm Tree** is an upright person in the middle and the other two making waving branches with their outstretched arms. The caller points to anyone in the circle calling out either Elephant or Palm Tree and the person pointed at is always the middle one and the two on either side, either ears or branches according to what is called. Another variation could be:

★ **'Stone, Tree and Water'** with appropriate action. An addition to Elephant and Palm Tree is to have a third category of monkeys in a row: 'Hear no evil, see no evil, speak no evil' or alternatively three bears one big, one medium and one tiny.

**Tossing the balls:** In a circle try to keep a ball in the air, then add another one and a third! The balls can vary in size. Balloons can also be used in the same way.

**Snap Action:** The group chooses 2 positions: eg. crosslegs, arms akimbo, or star position. In partners turn away from each other and it's snap if they both choose the same one, if not they try again. They can then change the ideas for positions or play it in threes and add sound to make it more complex, eg. kneeling and shouting 'Ho!' The important thing is that the children choose the actions.

**Sardines:** Hide and seek with one person hiding and the rest try to find her. As each one finds her they join to hide with her until everyone is there all squeezed together.

**Sleeping Lions:** All are lions frozen as if asleep, except for one who walks among the lions looking for anyone to move. As soon as anyone is caught they join in to help catch the others teasing is allowed, but no touching. Small children love this game.

**Balancing Co-operatively on Chairs:** The first person takes a firm chair and stands on it. The next one gives her chair to the first one, who puts it down next to her own. The second one then gets on the first one's chair in order to get to her own chair. The third one gives her chair to the first one who pasess it on to the second one who puts it down next to her. Then the third one gets on the first one's chair passes on to the second one's chair and arrives to stand on her own chair. The fourth one etc... and so on until everyone is standing on their chair in a circle. For young children it could be done with their small (firm!) chairs, or they could play it without moving any chairs, having placed them previously in a closely knit circle.

Thanks to Karen Coulthard for her idea.

★ **Free Association:** Choose a word and write it down and then draw a lot of bubbles coming from it writing inside each bubble the word that next comes into your mind; there can be a whole string of bubbles each joined up to the last one. This is a good beginning for creative writing.

**Spider's Web:** This is for a large group of people many of whom have a ball of string. The string is wound round everyone and then at a signal they all raise the string above their heads and it looks like an enormous spider's web.

**Twirligig:** Holding hands in a circle breaking at one point and then the leader goes round and round inside the circle until she is at the middle with all of the line holding hands and following her. When she gets to the middle she does an about-turn and continues until the original outside circle is back again.

# MORE CO-OPERATIVE GAMES

**Guess the Position:** one goes out, or two if preferred, and the group decide on a certain position, eg. they should sit back to back, or kneel etc. when they come in they try all sorts of positions and it is thumbs up or thumbs down, or 'Warmer, colder' clues, or clapping or humming loud or soft according to how near or far they are to the correct position.

**Tag Freeze:** if you are tagged you have to freeze until you are rescued by someone crawling through your legs. A variation is to balance a small cushion or bean bag on your head, or a homemade paper hat; if it falls off you have to freeze until someone picks it up for you still wearing their own gear.

**Elbow Tag:** in twos linking elbows; there are two catchers who can link on one side of any couple to make three and in that case the one on the other side is 'she' and has to try to catch the other loose one. Either catcher can always take refuge by linking on to a couple.

**Are You the Ghost?** Everyone wandering round, eyes closed, in a safe area. One is the ghost, but no one knows who, so you keep wandering round asking people softly 'Are you the Ghost?'. If they say 'No, I'm not the ghost', you go on asking someone else. If you do ask the ghost, he doesn't reply, so you join hands with him and carry on until there is just one big ghost. If this idea is frightening for small children, it could be something funny like a parrot or an Easter Rabbit.

**Moving Statues:** players get in line and the first one stands apart and makes a certain movement, like circling her arms, the second comes near and does another movement, eg. hopping round her and so with the third, etc. As a variation, sounds can be added. In the end it is like a big moving tableau.

**'Stand and face your loved one':** in a circle the caller stands in front of someone and everybody sings the title three times, ending with 'Before the break of day'. The one who has been chosen then takes the lead with the first one clutching her waist to the tune of 'Follow her to London' three times, ending with 'Before the Break of Day'. Make two small circles rather than having anyone waiting too long or have two people choosing and two lines going round. Modern versions of this traditional game are 'Taking the Train to London' where the 'train' asks the chosen one her name and they all say 'Hello' and her name three times. She then is the engine and goes on with her carriages to choose the next one to be asked their name.

**Winking:** in a circle the chosen first one winks at someone else and they have to change places. When they are used to this, someone can be placed in the middle of the circle to try to get to the vacant place before one of the others gets there. If he does, he is then the winker, if not, the one who has been winked at gets a turn to wink.

**Touch-a-Toe:** Everyone can have a turn with the tambourine to call out 'Touch a toe', 'an elbow', 'a knee' etc. or a colour or clothes. For older children they could call out a movement as well: 'Bunny jump with hands on ears!'

**Follow my Leader:** Everyone should have one turn as leader when the original leader goes to the back and the next one takes over.

**Follow the Group:** the group starts with everyone doing their own thing, without any leader, but aiming at all doing the same, eg. skipping, jumping on the spot.

# LARGE OUTDOOR FESTIVALS OR PARTIES

Many of the games described are suitable on a large scale. A new dimension in co-operative games has been introduced by organisations like Playfair in the form of parachutes and earth balls, described in many of the books listed in the Resources section. The parachute which has been manufactured in large quantities for war can be used for peaceful co-operation. They are sometimes to be obtained from ex-Army Stores or from Air Force Training Centres.

## What we can do:

**Parachute Activities:** Just holding it spread out at waist level can be an exciting experience, making it billow like waves on the ocean. This is quite an art and takes practice.

**Parachute!** Everyone stands holding the parachute and makes waves. When anyone shouts 'Parachute' they all raise their arms so that it billows above them. Only one turn each of shouting 'Parachute'.

**Mushroom.** A variation of this is where anyone can call out the name of any fruit or vegetable, until someone uses his one turn to call **'mushroom'**, and then, as in the call for 'parachute' they all raise it above their heads so that it billows in the air.

**Under the Parachute.** They can all sit inside the parachute after this billowing effect and keep it in position by sitting on the edge of the parachute and leaning against the 'walls'.

**Big Wheel.** Walking round holding the parachute at waist level, and gradually getting faster and faster until it is whirling; then gradually slow down to a full stop.

**Parachute Tag:** One is on top of the parachute and the other is underneath, the children holding the parachute at waist level. One is the catcher and the other the caught or the cat and the mouse. The rest of the children help whichever one they feel like. If the catcher is not making progress then he is helped and vice versa. The help is given by dropping the parachute to show where the cat or the mouse is hiding or creeping!

**Bouncing Balls.** A variety of bouncing balls can be used to circle round the parachute or alternatively to tip them off. The secret here is to be gentle and concentrate, as the balls seem to have a wilful will of their own!

# DOING THINGS TOGETHER

As a part of the co-operative scene there can be many examples of collaboration in learning experiences. These activities can help to restore the balance between co-operation and competition, at present so heavily weighted in favour of the competitive element. From an early age our youngsters are encouraged to pit themselves against their peers, particularly in the learning scene. "I'm on Book 5, you're only on Book 2" can be heard in the reception class for five year olds; yet they also have great capacities to help each other and to make their learning an exciting venture.

## What we can do:

**Group Murals and Collages:** Children in groups will decide to paint, paste or model a scene: a garden, the zoo, the seaside, the market, a farm, a village, etc.

**Group Freize:** similar themes on the wall.

**Group Jigsaws:** a large home-made picture cut up. Simple variations could be for 3, 4, or 5 people.

★ **Graffiti Board:** for drawings, jokes, riddles, ideas, opinions, etc.

★ **Imaginary Creatures:** made by group; then stories made up about their strange lives.

**Group Drama:** All drama is wonderfully co-operative and can often be combined with these ideas.

**Group Patchwork:** Each child makes a piece of patchwork knitted or sewn to attach to the rest. This can be done first with paper squares contributing to an overall pattern, each one pasting on her own coloured square or diamond.

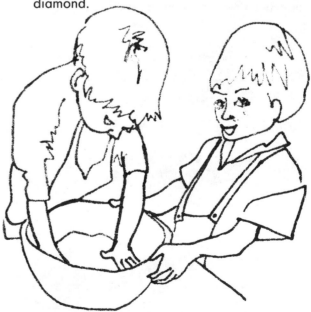

★ **Group Book:** Everyone contributing stories, poems, illustrations round a similar theme, or about the group itself.

★ **Group Silhouettes** arranged round the wall(s)

# LIFE AFFIRMING TOYS

So many toys in more affluent societies are now life-destroying rather than life-enhancing. It is no longer the case of toy guns or water pistols, but of deadly weapons and computer games whose one purpose is complete annihilation. This is just one more link in the socialisation of our children towards the acceptance of the inevitability of war and violence, a doctrine that is continually reiterated on television.

Fortunately children's natural powers of interest and curiosity have reacted to some extent against the crass monotony of the computer war games and there is a growing market for other computer activities, including sports and even some co-operative games. This does not alter the fact that most toy shops are full of the latest destructive weapons and parents are often at a loss to find something creative to give to their children, or whether to let them have their own choice, which, owing to media and peer group influence, usually ends in guns and military games as far as the boys are concerned. This is another argument for making your own toys and using all sorts of materials to hand, eg. packing cases.

A movement called 'Play for Life' is gaining ground in Britain and has its counterparts in many other countries; its aim is to promote life-enhancing toys through the manufacturers as well as the general public. These should be of good quality: something to appreciate and cherish rather than to throw away after the initial stimulation. They should also be peaceful and co-operative in essence, like many traditional games that provide alternatives to violence.

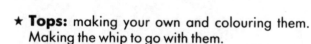

## What You Can Do:

Make your own toys, at first with help and encouragement from parents and teachers. These can range from simple sock puppets to home-made trucks and scooters. Simple games can be made up on a board with dice and counters: Homely versions of 'Snakes and Ladders', eg. 'The Big Picnic', with disasters and co-operation, or 'Exploration of the Planets', with many adventures on the way.

## Traditional Toys:

**Group Skipping:** all in together, running through, 'Salt, mustard, vinegar, pepper!' (double quick for pepper). Running under the rope, or taking one skip as one goes through.

★ **Tops:** making your own and colouring them. Making the whip to go with them.

★ **Hand top spinning:** in many countries this is a favourite skill.

**Kites:** make your own and colour them; have varieties, eg. birds, butterflies and moths. Have a kite run which is not a race.

**Musical Instruments:** home-made or from the shop: tambourines decorated with ribbons, drums, whistles, recorders, traditional instruments from faraway countries, castanets, etc.

**CHAPTER V** **GETTING ON WITH OTHERS**

Empathy
Understanding other Peoples
Interdependence
Anti-Racist Attitudes
Positive Gender Roles
Caring for the Planet
Futures

# EMPATHY: GETTING ON WITH OTHERS

All of us want to get on well with others and by working on our enhanced self-concept, our individual creativity and co-operative activities we stand a good chance of accepting others and being accepted. Mutual respect goes much further than courtesy and consideration, it is the complete freedom from domination that we should accord each other. This should not be interpreted as licence, it is rather the mutual accceptance of each other as reasonable human beings who can provide their own self-discipline and power.

## Activities:

★ **If I were you:** In partners get information about the other, eg. name, favourites (food, games, school lessons, etc.) and then one reports on the other pretending that it is herself. eg. 'My name is _____ I like _____

★ **Co-operative Jigsaws:** Groups of five can play this game. Each one in a group is given an envelope with jigsaw pieces that are all jumbled up but which will make five different animals all together. The game is to place your pieces right side up in front of you. There are three rules: no-one must talk; no-one may take a piece from another person, but you can give your pieces to others. The aim is to complete the five jigsaw animals and you can only do this by receiving pieces from your neighbours, never by taking them. When it is finished it is good to talk over with the children how they felt when they were longing to take a piece that they saw would fit into their jigsaw and make an animal. With smaller children there can be just two divisions of the animals. Cut out according to the drawings opposite or make up your own.

# UNDERSTANDING OTHER PEOPLES

It is said that children gradually become more receptive of other people throughout their childhood, reaching a maximum interest and openness by the age of twelve; thereafter, with the onset of puberty, they become more concerned with their own personal development and their previous attitudes tend to get consolidated. It is vital therefore to give them as much good experience of other cultures and different kinds of people as possible while they are young. It is a time too to work on their prejudices and enable them to sort out the reality about all of the many stereotypes they will have encountered. This should stand them in good stead when they emerge from adolescence to becoming caring and responsible citizens of the world.

## What we can do:

**Twinning:** between families or schools, at first locally and then further afield. Pictures, cards and photographs would be the most usual exchange, but some writing about daily lives by the older children will add to the picture of the similarities between all people, together with recognition of the differences.

**Imaginary Journey:** a dream sequence where you are taken on an imaginary journey to a country which is quite different from yours and which you like very much. You could describe and paint the country and the people.

**My Own Country.** Pack a bag, imaginary or real, of five things you would take to another country to show them what your country is really like.

**Photo Choice:** Choosing photographs that you like of a particular country, and with a partner decide on which you both like best, or alternatively, would like to know more about.

**Photo Questions:** Ask as many questions as possible about a photograph of a country and then try to find out the answers with help. It is always more interesting to include people in the photograph.

★ **Other Countries:** Read a story from another country and see if you can transpose it into another setting: eg. your own country or the past or the future or into space. What are the things that don't alter? This could then be developed as drama for older children.

# INTERDEPENDENCE

Only after much co-operative activity will it be possible for young children to grasp the wider concept of interdependence. Just as they need to know that milk does not just come from the supermarket, they can learn that all of the things they need for modern living: food, clothing and shelter come from someone else's hard work, often from people who have not enough of the essentials for living themselves. This knowledge will be tied up with unlearning common stereotypes such as white 'superiority' in an unequal world.

## What you can do:

Read or tell stories to mime or act: eg. **The Rainbow People:** This is another delightful story by Carolyn Askar about children who always play together happily until a stream of coloured ribbons comes down from the sky and they pick them up to wear: some red, some yellow, some green and some blue. A sharp wind descends on them and they huddle in their different corners. The reds have some matches but no sticks; the blues have sticks but no matches; the yellows have food but no water and the greens have water but no food. Then a tiny magic creature floats down to get them all contributing together!

## Act or Mime: The Greens and the Yellows,
a drama by Theatre Centre.

The Yellows live in the desert because the Greens have blocked off their river to make a dam for themselves. The Yellows hate the Greens and the Greens look down on the Yellows. One day an aeroplane belonging to the Greens crash lands in the Yellow desert and the Greens, after much mistrust, befriend the pilot and they discover that both sides are human beings and that they can help each other.

war is not healthy for children and other living things

# ANTI-RACIST ATTITUDES

It is surprising to many people how early young children take on the attitudes of the adults who care for them. It is the hidden messages that they pick up rather than any explicit discrimination, although there is often open prejudice, as for example, forbidding them to play with children from *that* family.

It is important to point out to children that all name calling is hurtful, but racist abuse of anyone is particularly horrible because it is part of the whole society's racism against black and brown people, and they are treated like second-class citizens just because their skin is of a different colour.

So we need to provide opportunities to counter this stereotyping, with plenty of experience of different cultures, to learn that all people, whatever the colour of their skin, have the same basic individuality. Stories, films, and TV programmes should be found that reflect a good cross-section of humanity instead of depicting a wholly white world with a stereotyped or token 'black'.

Ann Constanti

## ACTIVITIES.

**Stop the Racist Name Calling.** Choose or make up the beginning of a story about a child who is being bullied in the playground because she is black. Brainstorm what can be done about it with an adult (later when the process is well practised the children can do this on their own). Choose as a group one or more of the best solutions. There can be many versions of this problem which can also be acted out as a role play.

★ **Purple Badges:** Half the children have a purple badge pinned on them for half a day or less. This means they are 'second class citizens' and are treated as such, disparaging them and saying things like, 'That's what you would expect from the purple badge people'. Swop over and discuss how they felt. This can be a painful exercise and should only be attempted for a short time in an environment that has a really stable and secure atmosphere. It is based on the well-known 'Eye of the Storm' film listed in the resource section.

# POSITIVE GENDER ROLES

Many conflicts stem from problems between the sexes or their gender roles and much of this originates in childhood. Children as well as adults can have fixed ideas about what little boys are supposed to be like and that little girls are set in a totally different image, and this all takes place well before they are five years old. In fact much that has been said about racial discrimination can apply to sexist attitudes and here the experience is common to almost all societies, some more divisive than others. We know that it is common for adults to give more attention to the boys, and the girls usually get the rawest deal; but also the boys, whose upbringing often deprives them of expressing their most sensitive and caring feelings. A movement against this sex-role stereotyping is gaining ground, but we still have to go a long way before it is generally accepted that 'little boys *can cry*' and 'little girls can be just as adventuresome as little boys'.

So both boys and girls need to explore their prejudices and discrimination with regard to sexism, and this can be done at an early age. Again stories, films and TV programmes can be chosen to counter some of this sexism; they can depict the wide range of possibilities for both sexes and should be a part of the provision in the home and the school; unfortunately they are still thin on the ground, so it is particularly necessary to go on developing an awareness of sex-stereotyping in the media, literature and everyday life.

## What we can do.

**Talk:** Discuss what they watch and read from an anti-sexist point of view. eg. Is is always the boys who are the leaders and initiators?

**Photo Surprise:** Use photographs showing men and women, girls and boys with unexpected gender roles. eg. men ironing, women driving a bus, boys making a bed, girls playing football. Talk about them, make up stories about them.

# FUTURES

How do we prepare children for the future? It is true that this is a concept that is very gradually developed and we should realise that for small children the future is very vague and remote. However, we can begin with descriptions of what they will do in the week-end and holidays. In a gradual progression they can become more and more aware of themselves in relation to the past, present and future. This is important for them: it gives perspective and a realisation of the changing world about them. In its turn this gives rise to an awareness of one's own ability to change things and the possibility of making life better.

## What we can do.

**All about me:** A notebook from birth until the present day, with photographs and illustrations.

**Time Line.** Draw a line across a wide paper and on the line draw something very special that happened to you. In pairs or small groups share what it was.

★ **Life Line** As above, draw in several important things that happened to you. Mark out your number of years, getting help if necessary, and put arrows linking the drawing to your age when it happened. eg. moved house 10 years old.

★ **Future Lines.** Carry on the line until you are grown up. What sort of things might happen to you?

★ **Future World.** What would you like the world to be when you are grown up? Draw a picture of what you would like it to be like. What do you think it would really be like? Draw a picture of this too.

# CARING FOR THE PLANET

It is easier to show young children the value of caring for the planet than it is to enable them to feel they can do anything to prevent nations going to war; and we must not ignore the fact that the planet Earth is in grave danger of being destroyed, not only by the threat of nuclear warfare, but also through the pollution and the devastation of its natural resources.

From small activities such as planting a tree (and even in the most overcrowded cities there are tree-planting schemes) to learning about the disappearance of the tropical rain forests, with dire consequences for the climate of the world, we can lay the foundation for future citizens, who will prevent further deterioration of our precious 'homeland'.It is true that industrialisation brings benefits of material comforts such as electricity and water supplies, and these are now necessities and should be available to everyone; but the dilemma is that it also brings in its wake a package way of living, complete with pollution and 'throw away' goods. Young children cannot be expected to understand all of these complexities, but they can appreciate ideas of sharing and caring for nature as well as for people, and of course the two are mutually dependent.

## What we can do.

Joining the 'Plant a Tree' in the town.

**Window sill** planting – everything from mustard and cress to bulbs and flowers; also pot plants and flowers.

**Group Plan** of a playground, garden, village or town – a desert island community.

**Re-cycling activities.** Bottles and paper.

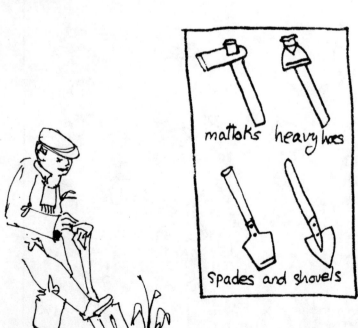

mattoks   heavy hoes

spades and shovels

★ **Pollution.** Older children could find examples of pollution in their neighbourhood, and take some action.

★ **Spaceship.** For a long journey into space what would you want to take? What might you have to leave behind if you could only take three personal things?

**Flood.** Draw a picture of yourself at home with your favourite belongings around you. There is a flood and you have time only to take three things. What would you choose?

★ **Endangered Species** – find out with adults' help about any plants or animals, that are endangered, such as orchids, bats, whales and tigers, and find out what we can do about it.

### CHAPTER VI      PEACEFUL CONFLICT-SOLVING

Dealing with Fears of Violence, War and Death
Fairness and Justice
Empowerment
Peaceful Conflict-Solving

# FAIRNESS AND JUSTICE

Probably the most common sentence used by all children is "Tisn't fair!"; and we are often tempted to reply, 'Nothing's fair', from the superior adult point of view. Yet they are generally right and we should really be thankful that they have this inherent sense of justice to draw on. It is sometimes hard for us parents and teachers to live up to this moral stance, (always in their favour!), but it provides a basis for mutual discussion as to how, between us, we can come to an agreement, bearing in mind everyone's need for justice.

This whole book has been concerned with fairplay and justice, which is the essence of co-operation. One could say that affirmation is both doing oneself justice and giving the same sort of recognition to others. All of the aspects of communication are concerned with giving everyone a fair chance to speak and a fair hearing. Again empathy towards other people is concerned with whether they have a fair deal. One could say in fact that all of the activities in this book are basically to do with fairplay and justice.

## What we can do.

All the activities in this book!

**Fair Ways of Choosing Somebody for a Game.** It is often a problem for adults when one or two children have to be chosen and we have all experienced a mass of eager faces all waiting to be chosen. But children have always had their own methods of resolving this problem by rhymes and counting games, like, 'One potato, two potatoes,' etc., and we can follow their example rather than booster our position as arbitrators. We could use their's, often handed down over the generations, or we could make up some new ones together. We could also draw lots: slips of paper in a hat with three marked 1, 2 and 3 respectively. Those who have the marked slips can have 1st, 2nd and 3rd choice at being the leader. Next time they will not draw. This little operation can be organised by quite young children.

**Fixing the Rules:** We could learn how children do make up their own rules. For example, there are some very complex ones for games of marbles and conkers. We can then make up new games and decide with them about the rules. One very important factor is that smaller children are inclined to believe that rules are inflexible and it is good for them to learn that they can be changed if everyone agrees, and this can provide variety and invention.

# DEALING WITH FEARS OF VIOLENCE, WAR AND DEATH

With young children the most important factor is to provide the secure atmosphere that will enable them to voice their fears and their guilt, as they often feel that any catastrophe might be due to some of their own uncontrollable passions.

It is well known now that many children, even the young ones, are aware that the 'bomb' could blow us all to pieces. Even with adults this subject is usually unmentionable; 'inconceivable' in fact; so it is doubly important for the children to ask about it if they need to. This does not mean that adults should initiate these fears; when the time comes there will be questions about war and the bomb together with the whole range of their insatiable curiosity.

Very young children need to be reassured that their adult figures are able to cope, and all children need to know that we are not helpless in matters of peace and war, and we must also be convinced that we are not completely helpless. What we do about it will vary from democratic action or protests to vigils or prayer, and what we give to our children will be largely ourselves as models: our example of peacefulness and belief in our power as citizens will be the best heritage we can give to them.

Death with its inevitability has been very much a taboo subject in modern society, and this has been particularly harmful to children as the prohibition increases their fears and prevents open supportive discussion. Fortunately there is a growing tendency to be more open about death and this could greatly improve family relationships in particular, as even if there is no direct experience of death, it is very much in young children's minds, especially the idea of their parents dying, and frank and open talk can ease their fears.

## Pictures of Peace and War

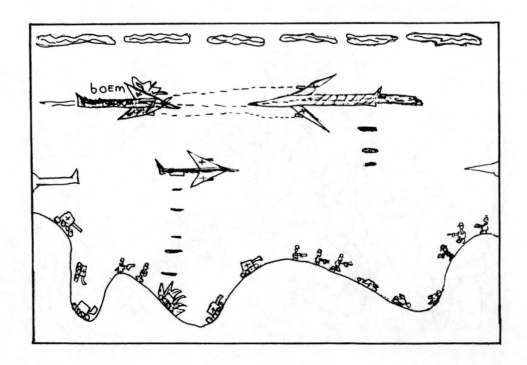

wednesday June 13th Ross Johnson when I am angry I say you better go away or I will hit you. I Feel Like hurting them.

# EMPOWERMENT

This quality is born out of affirmation and a good self-concept on the one hand and the ability to co-operate on the other, and it is a basic ingredient for peaceful conflict-solving. We are in fact educating children to their own power and supporting them as they grow up to use their power wisely and with consideration for others. Co-operation enables children to see what a friendly group of people can achieve together; these may only be little ripples but the overall result can be that they feel positive about their power to make changes rather than feeling hopeless in the face of authority. This is the sort of power that can give great strength to the individual and give them a feeling of the support of the whole group.

There is a natural theme of empowerment throughout young children's fantasies and imaginative play. The giants, the monsters and now the popular dinosaurs are grappled with, so that the children will be better able to deal with their own powerful adult figures by releasing their emotions in a harmless way. In fact the whole tradition of fairy tales and myths enables those who are weak to attain positions of strength and fulfillment. The important thing is to be able to channel these aspirations along positive and non-destructive lines.

## What we can do.

**We're on Top of the Castle:** if you are lucky enough to have an Earth Ball, (a blow-up ball of about one metre in diameter) the game of 'I'm the king of the castle' can be transformed into seeing how many children can balance on the top of it, helping each other to stay there. (Safety precautions needed for small children.) If you haven't got a ball of that size, which is more than likely, it is possible to devise 'castles' such as benches, or a low safe table.

**To the Rescue:** A series of incidents where the younger children rescue their adults (parents or teachers) from danger: eg. they have fallen down a cliff and have to be hauled up by everyone helping. For older children these improvisations could include such adventures as discovering smugglers, caught in the act! Or a space ship gets stranded on a planet where the children are in charge. They have to decide whether they will help the crew, who have no food or water.

## Improvisations:

There are many dramatic improvisations that can foster empowerment, in fact children's stories are full of them. We can invent our own.

**Interview:** The teacher or one of the more powerful and confident children can be interviewed for a very lowly job. The timid ones can form the interviewing panel.

**Please!** eg. The parents can ask a very special favour of their children. Some people are coming to stay and need their room; can they have camp beds? They want to watch a special programme on television at the time the children have their own favourite.

# PEACEFUL CONFLICT SOLVING

The end result of practising all of the activities so far listed could be that we are now all primed to solve our conflicts peacefully! That would be ideal, but we might well be a few steps nearer to this. The essential fact is to realise that there are many different ways to resolve conflicts, besides the extremes of aggression or submission, neither of which are usually successful in reaching a mutually acceptable solution. In fact, submission can have serious repercussions when anger has been repressed and finally bursts out as explosive violence. It is worth exploring the possibilities of assertion techniques, which can be effective in so far as the other party can get a clear, calm picture of your point of view, at the same time as being reassured that you will listen to his/her side of the question. Yes, idealistic when dealing with young children, but when one considers that the aggressive or the submissive stance does not solve the problem, but usually perpetuates it and makes it worse in the long run, it is worth trying other approaches.

Assertion techniques depend on the hope that both parties fully understand the situation and will work at coming to some kind of an agreement or compromise. The best to hope for is a win/win solution where both parties are satisfied with the result.

## What we can do:

★ **Detectives:** Other children watching groups of nursery or infant children at play. They discuss afterwards the causes of conflicts and ways in which they were 'resolved', (usually by fighting or retreat, discussion and negotiation, or arbitration by someone else, usually an adult). They then decide whether these were the best solutions and what they would have preferred.

**Video Detectives:** as above but watching short videos. Even younger children can do this for a short time with guidance.

Everyone will have their own ideas about sanctions and discipline, and this book makes a plea for mutual respect and responsibilities, which entail discussion and working out peaceful solutions so that the good relationships are not impaired or put at risk.

Jenny Humm wednesday June 13th
When you are angry you shout and get very cross and you might hit somebody. I feel I should go and tell mummy.

**Yes! No!:** In partners, one saying 'Yes' all the time and the other saying 'No'. There can be variations in persuading; tone of voice, loud/soft etc. Similarly with:

**'It's raining!' 'No, it isn't!':** 'The sun's shining', 'No, it isn't!' These two are one-minute warm-ups!

**Arguing:** 'Which colour is best?' in pairs. Of course there is no right answer. Between a knife and a fork: which is more useful? One pretends to be a knife and the other a fork – then change.

**Hassle Lines:** Line up with a partner and take it in turns to role play a situation: eg, someone grabs a tricycle or scooter just as you are getting on; someone knocks down your paint box by mistake; a parent is hitting a little child, you protest and tell the parent to stop; the parent refuses.

**Desert Island :** you are all shipwrecked on a desert island without your grown-ups. How do you manage? Who will do what? This is a good setting for role-play and simulated (or real) conflicts to work out.

✳ ✳ ✳ ✳ ✳ ✳ ✳

**Hand Quarrel:** As above, but using one hand each instead of an instrument. The hand could be shaped like a bird or donkey or shadows of hands could be used.

**Cat and Dog Fight** Tell all the different ways in which you would stop *your* cat and dog from fighting; e.g. feed them in different rooms (prevention); pour cold water on them (if it happens!); bring them up together from the beginning. Discuss the various solutions.

**Musical Quarrel:** Two people with a musical instrument: (zylophones, castanets, drums, etc.) each can start a 'conversation' of sounds, one playing to begin and the other replying. This gradually becomes a quarrel. Can you then make it up and become friends again? Older children could try acting it out in several different ways. Which was the best?

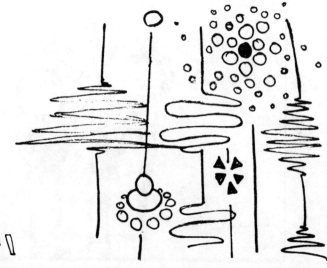

# What we can do:

★ **Group Picture Ranking:** 4 or more attractive and varied pictures are on display, each person selects them in order of preference, either by number or a simple sketch or on a slip of paper, whispering 1st choice to the leader in the case of younger children. The slips are posted into a 'letter-box' and can be used as a graph later. Make up small groups and have a set of identical pictures in each group and the group tries to rank them in order of preference, which means a lot of give and take. If this is too difficult they could try to agree on their first choice.

fighting with my Mummy.

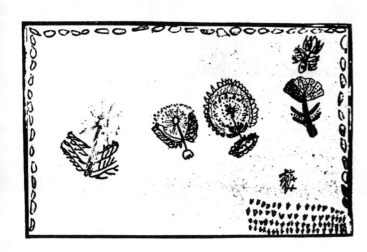

# PEACEFUL CONFLICT SOLVING

**Two Donkeys:** Cut out the six shapes in the cartoon opposite and get couples to put them in order. Make up a story about them. Mime it with sounds and then act out with words. Try it again pretending they are dogs, cows, pigs. Mime it with sounds.

Quaker Peace & Service

# CONFLICT SOLVING

## Actual quarrels and anti-social behaviour.

The keynote is always to try to bring the tension down and to try to prevent escalation. Just as in the political world retaliation and revenge exacerbate the situation, so if you hit back harder the conflict worsens – you might get as 'good' as you gave or you might 'win' if the other party cannot hit back, but no sort of a permanent peaceful solution can be resolved that way. Likewise when adults apply physical sanctions and slap or hit they are not getting to the heart of the matter, which is to resolve the conflict so that both sides are as reasonably satisfied as possible. They have certainly shown where the power lies and therefore who is powerless; they have also provided an unspoken example of 'might is right', which will be duly copied should the occasion arise. (Note I am not referring to physical restraint where a child would be in danger, eg, stopping a toddler from putting inquisitive fingers into electric plugs or holding a distraught child firmly to prevent him doing damage to others).

## Role-playing in Everyday Conflicts:

Choose a situation such as one child has lost her pen and she sees one like it on another boy's desk. She takes it and the boy threatens to hit her if she doesn't give it back; or alternatively two children are building a big castle with bricks and their small brother wants to knock it down every time. They could brainstorm what might happen next. They could then take on different roles and set them out with an adult's help if necessary. The use of puppets is ideal here.

## Family role-play:

take one card each without looking at it. Each card has a family word on it like, Mother, Father, Brother, Grandmother, Auntie, etc. and if you pick yourself, choose another card, although you could keep it in the sense that you could be both an auntie and a sister. The group can then decide on a problem or be given one and they try to solve it along the steps indicated above. The important thing about role-play is the discussion afterwards. What did it feel like? A similar theme can be done in the school setting: teachers, head, parents, dinner ladies, etc.

when i am angry I feel cross and I feel cross with my sister Rachel and she makes me very cross and I have to shout to her and I feel all horrible in my tummy.

## Co-operative Role-Play:

The children decide on a conflict that happens to them frequently. eg. an adult pushes past them at the bus stop: a bigger child wants to borrow their bicycle and they don't trust him with it; each one wants a different programme on television. Two volunteers act it out in front of the rest. Anyone can tap one of them on the shoulder and take his place and try to get to a win/win solution, by asserting, rather than using aggression or giving in unwillingly. Discuss afterwards where there was aggression, assertion or reluctant submission.

★ **Problem phone-in:** in two groups, each group thinks of a problem and tapes it. They exchange tape recorders and brainstorm solutions choosing the one or ones they like best. This activity can also be done in writing.

★ **Dear Auntie Joy:** letters to Auntie Joy saying they have a problem and describing it briefly. Small groups take one letter out of the post box and decide what they will reply.

**Steps in Conflict-solving:** 1. What is the solution? What happened? Could it be role-played? 2. Each one expresses her own feelings saying honestly how they feel. If only one of the parties is there the group should elicit what they think the other party would be feeling. 3. Brainstorming what we think might happen and also what we would like to happen. 4. There should then be a group decision as to what action could or should be taken. This section should be planned out step by step.

This is Laura

This is he

my friend plays with me she playc with me a lot.

Nicola

**Real Conflicts** One can only put forward tentative rules of thumb such as: count up to ten; keeping it cool, preventing physical violence; mediating by listening to each in turn; getting children to repeat what the other one said; getting older children to 'sit on the step' on some chosen peacemaking place and work it out themselves and come back when it is settled.

# BIBLIOGRAPHY

*All about Me,* Teachers' Guide, Schools Council Health Education Project, Nelson 1977.

*Art Games and Structures for Groups,* Marion Liebman, Bristol.

*Between Parent and Child,* Haim Ginott, NY Avon, 1969.

*The Changing World and the Primary School,* Barbara Clark et al. CWDE 1979.

*Childhood and Society,* Erik Erikson, Pelican.

*The Children We Teach,* Susan Isaacs, University of London Press 1965.

*Conflict Change and Our Future,* Ely Resource and Technology Centre, Cambs.

*Co-operative Games,* PEP Talk, No 7. Autumn 1985. Peace Education Project Journal, Peace Pledge Union.

*Creative Listening,* Rachel Pinney 1981

*Dibs in Search of Self,* Virginia Axeline, Ballantine Books 1969.

*Doing Things in and about the House.* Photographs and Activities about Work, Play and Equality, Serawood House,1983.

*Drama, A Learning Experience,* B. Wagner, Hutchison.

*Education for Liberation,* Adam Curle, Tavistock 1979.

*The Experience of Parenthood,* Chris Buckton, Longman, 1980

*Freedom to Learn,* Carl Rogers, Charles Merrill, 1985.

*Games Children Play around the World,* John Adams Toys Ltd. 1979.

*Getting to Yes,* Roger Fisher & William Ury, Hutchison 1983.

*Growing in Peace,* Produced by Pax Christi.

*How Children Fail,* John Holt, Pelican.

*How Children Learn,* John Holt, Pelican.

*How to Talk so Kids Will Listen,* Adele Faber & Elaine Mazlish, Avon 1980

*How to Teach Peace to Children,* J. Lorne Peachey, Herald Press, 1981.

*Interpersonal Skills,* Patrick Whitaker.

*Introductory Manual for Peace Education.* Manchester Peace Education Group, Gil Isaacson & Georgeanne Lamont, 1985.

*Learning for Change in World Society,* Robin Richardson, World Studies 1976.

*Lifeskills Teaching Programmes,* B. Hopson & M Scally, Lifeskills Associates, 1981.

*Origins of Love and Hate,* Ian Suttie, Routledge 1935, Penguin1963.

*A Manual of Non-Violence and Children,* S.Judson et al. Philadelphia, 1982.

*Peace Games and Drama,* Peace Education Newsletter,1984.

*Peace Education Guidelines for Primary Secondary Schools,* Avon c.c. 1982.

*Personal Power,* Carl Rogers, Constable, 1978.

*Playing and Reality,* D.W. Winicott, Tavistock 1971,Pelican1974.

*Psychological Aspects of Child Development.* Pamphlet by Susan Isaacs.

*A Repertoire of Peacemaking Skills,* Susan Carpenter. Consortium on Peace Research Education and Development, 1977.

*Sharing Nature With Children,* Joseph Bharat Cornell, Exley Publications 1979.

*The Slant of the Pen,Racism in Children's Books,* Roy Preirwerk, World council of Churches.

*Spirit of Fire,* Carolyn Askar, Element Books 1983.

*Stories for Guided Fantasy,* Carolyn Askar, High Warren , Barnet Lane,Elstree, Herts.
*Summerhill,* A.S..Neill, Pelican.
*Teacher,* Sylvia Aston Warner.
*Teaching Children to Love Themselves,* Michael Knight et al. Spectrum 1982.
*Theatre Centre Teachers' Notes,* Theatre Centre, Hanover School, London.
*Tinderbox,* Sylvia Barratt & Sheena Hodge, 66 Songs for Children, A&C Black 1982.
*Two Worlds of Childhood,* US and USSR, Urie Bronfenbrenner, Touchstone 1970.
*What is a Family?* Development education Centre, Birmingham 1985.
*Winners All,* Pax Christi 1979.
*Whole Child/Whole Parent,* Polly Berrien Berends, Harper & Row 1983.
*The World in Birmingham,*Photopack. Development Education Centre, Selly Oak
Colleges, Birmingham 1982.
*World Studies, 8-13.* A Teachers' Handbook. S.Fisher & D. Hicks, Oliver & Boyd 1985.

## Books for Children

Beans Series:*Pakistani Village,Chun Ling in China, Sri Lanka & Village in Egypt,*
A&C Black.
*House by Mouse,* George Mendoza, Deutsch 1982.
*How They Live Now* Series, Lutterworth 1980.
*How We Feel; How We Work; How We Live and How We Play,*  A. Harper & C. Roche,
Kestrel.
*Moose,* Michael Foreman, Picture Puffin 1973.
*The Peace Book,* Bernard Benson, Jonathon Cape 1980.
*The Story of Ferdinand,* Munro Leaf, Puffin1977.
*The Turbulent Team of Tyke Tiler,* Gene Kemp, Penguin 1977.
*Wacky and his Fuddlejig,* Stanford Summers, Arts in Context 1981.

## Films and Filmstrips

*The Eye of the Storm.*  A Film or Video on Prejudice, Concord.
*Toys.*  A film taking the idea of war toys to its logical conclusion, Concord.
*Unlearning Indian Stereotypes.*  Council for Inter-racial Books for Children, N.Y.
*Winners and Losers,* Oxfam.